Take a Look Again...

A unique anthology of poems and
musical lyrics, shared by
five generations.

*Compiled by Annette-Frances B.
and David King*

Collection and notes copyright © Annette-Frances B. and David King 2020

Poems and musical lyrics copyright © remains with the individual poets and lyricists

Cover design copyright © John O'Shea 2020
Photographs copyright © John O' Shea 2020

Moral rights asserted.
All rights reserved. No part of this publication maybe reproduced, stored in a retrieval system, or transmitted, in any form or by any means electronic, mechanical, photocopying, recording or otherwise, without the prior written permission of the publisher.

Whilst every effort has been made to ensure that any information and general knowledge within in this book was correct at press time, the authors and publisher do not assume and hereby disclaim any liability, to any person or persons, for any loss, damage or disruption caused by inaccuracies or omissions, whether such inaccuracies or omissions result from negligence, accident or any other origin.

ISBN 978-0-9935564-8-7

Published in the UK by:

Louannvee Publishing
www.louannveepublishing.co.uk

Dedicated to

Vera Annie Webb – Née Way

Your beautiful spirit...
lives on, inspires, prevails and triumphs
within our hearts
forever…

Acknowledgements

We would like to thank everyone for allowing us to include their poems / song lyrics within this book and John O'Shea whose photographs add depth and beauty to the contents and cover. Thank you.

CONTENTS

Living or Existing?

Alex Louis Way Brannon *Oasis* 1
Alex Louis Way Brannon *Take a Look Again* 2
Alex Louis Way Brannon *Before You Know it, You're Somewhere Else* 4
Alex Louis Way Brannon *A Momentary Snapshot* 5
Alex Louis Way Brannon *What is…* 7
R. W. Brannon *Where is Time if Not Forgotten?* 8
Tom B. *S**t Kickers Bargain Bucket* 10
Vera Annie Webb…Née Way *Life* 12
Vera Annie Webb…Née Way *Summer Thoughts* 13

Space and Nature

Annette-Frances B. *Morning Awakes* 15
Annette-Frances B. *Forgotten* 15
Annette-Frances B. *Favourite Place* 16
Vera Annie Webb…Née Way *Little Bird* 16
Vera Annie Webb…Née Way *Sights and Sounds I Love* 17
Vera Annie Webb…Née Way *Dandelions and Buttercups* 18
Vera Annie Webb…Née Way *Winter Scene* 19
A. D. Brannon *What If?* 20
Alex Louis Way Brannon *Still Moving I Sat* 22

Peace not War

Alex Louis Way Brannon *Why?* 25
Vera Annie Webb…Née Way *Song* 26
R. W. Brannon *Look into the Eyes of Humanity* 27
Griffin E. D. Way *General War* 28
Vera Annie Webb…Née Way *We Cannot Change the World* 30
Vera Annie Webb…Née Way *People* 31
Tom B. *Betrayer's Voice* 32
Tom B. *Thermo Nuclear Twister* 35
Annette-Frances B. *Nuclear Weapons – War…* 38
Vera Annie Webb…Née Way *I Think About the World* 39

Freedom or Oppression?

Tom B. *Welcome to the GAHC!* 41
Tom B. *Cliché* 43
S. A. W. Brannon *Hypocrite Boogie* 44
Annette-Frances B. *Omega* 45
Annette-Frances B. *Fleeting Glimpse* 47
Alex Louis Way Brannon *Survival of the Fittest* 48

Work and Routine

Annette-Frances B. *The Manager Saves the Day* 51
Annette-Frances B. *Always Purchase Your Car Tax on Time* 52
Tom B. *Vicious Cycle* 54
Tom B. *+ Directional Hard Work* 56
R. W. Brannon *Supermarket Chaos* 59
David King *Resolutions* 62
David King *Inventions* 63
David King *Paradox* 64
Alex Louis Way Brannon *As Morning Tones* 66
Annette-Frances B. *First Flat – Somewhere in Muswell Hill* 67

Relationships

Vera Annie Webb…Née Way *Parted* 69
David King *Poetical Reflections* 70
David King *My One and Only Vera* 71
L. A. Brannon *Nobody in the World* 72
R. W. Brannon *Toast to Our Love* 72
S. A. W. Brannon *If I Lived a Million Times* 73
Annette-Frances B. *To my Father* 74
Annette-Frances B. *Do You Like Italian Opera?* 74
Annette-Frances B. *Our Dream* 75
Annette-Frances B. *Message from Annette* 76
S. A. W. Brannon *Our Grandma* 77
Annette-Frances B. *Beautiful Spirit* 78
David King *The Rest is Just the Past* 79
David King *To Vera* 80
David King *People Lanterns* 80

Fleeting Thoughts

Vera Annie Webb…Née Way *Now but a Memory* 83
Griffin E. D. Way (Griff) *Wise Words* 83
Alex Louis Way Brannon *Where am I and how did I get here?* 84
Jack Ray Louis Brannon *My Hand in Yours* (Pictorial) 85

NOTES

Links Between Writers

86—87

Brief Biographies

Griffin E. D. Way 89
Vera Annie Webb - Née Way 90
David King 91
Annette-Frances B. 92
R. W. Brannon 92
Alex Louis Way Brannon 93
A. D. Brannon 93
Tom B. 94
S. A. W. Brannon 94
L. A. Brannon 94

INDEX

Writers 95
Titles and First Lines 96 - 99

Living or Existing?

Oasis *(Composed 2003)*

We all walk the desert
grey, monotone, parched dry.
The meeting of ground to sky.
Beyond the scanning,
probing, searching, waning eye
harsh perception,
we lust for water.
Even one tear to sooth our feet.
The foot prints a tiny softening resonance,
washed away by the numbing wind
and the perpetual driving rhythm,
like a drum, pounding the sand.
Nothing, just sky and ground…

I was led by the sound of a bird,
glistening like the jewel of a single planet.
Led,
to a place,
a beautiful place.
It took my hand and for a moment,
I was sitting by a river,
the water soothing, quenching, healing my feet,
like the wash of the sun,
in sunrise over a darkened land.
A place of pure colour, sound, emotion.
The lush green, the blue sky, the warmth of the sun…
The rolling hills, the drifting birds…
The gentle, silent trees.
A place with no limits.
It was nothing.
It was everything.
Personal, but real.

A forgotten place,
like a children's playground…
A place beyond words,
where you are free and in touch with yourself.
A place you swear you will never leave,
but the desert is back as if it had never left,
your familiar reality.

I awoke, the pen fell from my hands
and I walked onwards.

We all walk the desert and stagger and crawl.
We can all find the oasis,
when we stop looking
and start seeing.

ALEX LOUIS WAY BRANNON

Take a Look Again *(Composed 2003)*

We all stop counting after a while.
Awareness slips away like a 'thief in the night'…

Sky becomes cloud,
cloud becomes sea.
Sea becomes river,
rivers become trees,
trees become concrete.

Emotion becomes words,
words become phrases.

Phrases become clichés,
clichés become amusement.
Amusement becomes jest,
jest becomes bullying.
Bullying becomes anger,
anger becomes hatred.

Friends become fond memories,
fond memories become echoes.
Echoes become names,
names are forgotten.

And before you know it,
you're standing so far down the road,
you have even lost yourself!
You're sitting in a rocking chair,
surrounded by things you didn't even want,
watching people fly past on rocket ships,
wondering how you arrived there.

Take a look again.

ALEX LOUIS WAY BRANNON

Before You Know it,
You're Somewhere Else *(Composed 2003)*

I close my eyes, for a second.
Every time I open them again
I am somewhere else, for but a moment.
From place to place the unstoppable river just goes on.
You have those seconds though,
that momentary time, when you stop,
to see, to believe.
You gaze up at the new canopy above you,
watching the light drift down, through the holes,
like stars riding on the backs of feathers.
The bird songs, like whispers,
dance around the fire within your soul.
Torrential tears flood the grounds,
tears of a baby in a new world,
tears of sadness,
then tears for tears
and tears for joy.
Then off, off, off…
I drift again,
the surging river of being,
embracing, eyes closed,
I drift,
arms outstretched, on a raft of trust,
with sails of faith
and the food of hope,
to just be,
until it all becomes the river,
even you.

Before you know it you're somewhere else, again,
                                    for a moment.

Sometimes,
sometimes, when you stop,
there are thousands of people, hanging from trees above,
locked in fear,
scared of drowning,
or being caught on rocks,
hanging like fruit…

ALEX LOUIS WAY BRANNON

A Momentary Snapshot *(Composed year 2003)*

How can state be different
if it is just a momentary snapshot
of an ever-changing journey?
In fact, everything is connected,
in one great relationship.
Everything is part of everything else
and eventually will become everything else.
Anger and fear are misheard love.
You must know - everything evolves one way or another,
things don't just cease to be,
they change.
Every word you speak,
every look, every glance,
every face you pull,
is passed on to someone,
then, in turn, is passed to someone else
and before you know what's what,
a sweet smile, you smiled, has travelled the earth –
really,
it is all just love.

We forge things,
define their use and forms,
but the irony is,
our compulsive control lasts but a second.

We seem to hold on to things.
Moments become obsessively precious,
until we are sitting in a room that's a shrine to our past
and that's all we have.
Too scared to embrace the future,
too scared to come down, from the tree we are gripping on to.
We hold things close to us
and protect them.
The future becomes an extension of the past,
it becomes preconceived, based on experiences.
We begin to make decisions, based on those experiences,
only allow ourselves to repeat things that we have already
found happiness around.
And so, this goes on,
until we cut ourselves off from so much
that we live in a micro-perception of the world,
making our world smaller and smaller,
until it destroys the things that were good.
Take a step out, away from the front door…
It's spring again,
but it's a new spring,
it's different this time.
It's always different,
things never stop moving,
they constantly change…
To define is to deny,
to explain is to perceive,
but to be blind is to see.

ALEX LOUIS WAY BRANNON

What is... *(Composed 2003)*

Carve the world up, for ease of manipulation…
A whirl wind of pseudo clarity,
churning through all that does not fit.
A sanitation,
a fresh coat
 of white light.

We are told microbes are small,
the ground is hard,
the rain is wet,
trees stand still,
the sky is blue,
the sun is a burning ball of gas,
there's a vast universe out there
and time is always constant.

Here is what's wrong and what's right,
choose from this tray of seeds, like comfort food.
It's all laid out for us,
the mapped arena of reality.

It's all about seeing…
Gold to one man may be shackles to another.

It's all just a perception,
a constant, changing reflection,
of yourself,
bound by consciousness,
tainted by experience
and defined by society.

But, what's beyond the whitewash?
But, what's beyond the tray,
beyond the eyes,
beyond the conscious,
beyond the explanation,
beyond the obsessive grip of holding on?

Sometimes, I feel I'm standing on the head of a pin,
claustrophobic,
crushed by definition and control.
In a vacuum that is induced by the fear of letting go.
But, to let go is to see…
To see the rainbow of rich, pure colour.
To allow yourself to drift,
to simply be, without question.

ALEX LOUIS WAY BRANNON

Where is Time if Not Forgotten? *(Composed 2014)*

Capture the moment in time,
like a camera…
That moment in time has gone,
yet there it is before you,
or are we wrong?
You can replay it,
over and over again, exactly the same.
It defies time long gone.
A moving image, a spoken word,
defying the right to be there.

What a privilege to see the past,
like a God viewing the universe.
That time has gone,
along with the living,
Yet - there it is,
it lives on…
How does it affect those who watch it?

Is time something we leave behind,
something we've lost,
a mere measurement of movement,
as in sun rise, sun set,
or perhaps something more?
Is three pm today
captured within the same space
as three pm tomorrow and
three pm yesterday?
If so,
why can we not stand within that same time?
Or do we?

R. W. BRANNON

(Extract from the musical lyrics composed 1998)

S**T KICKERS BARGAIN BUCKET

NO SPACE
FOR TIME
NEED TIME
FOR SPACE
WHEN ALL
DEFINE
DEFEND
DISGRACE

New improved
another version of the truth.
2 4 1
this diversion for your use
interlude
in the emersion of life
no conclusion
in that perversion of proof.

Through the glistening red salvation of a thousand, to endless
unfulfilled,
skin torn, passion worn, a new s**t storm, for the anti-norm.
Ye-ya we are the skinless,
never to be seen, acknowledgment just a distant dream,
above the skies our phantom flies,
its physical embodiment a darkened mist,
its thought in swaths, this beast behaves
for no man.

It climbs, it takes, it cannot break,
its voice it shakes a lightning chase,
struck flame of hate, speeding blood awake
to the sound in the veins below,
as the intent in their eyes grow,
like seeds of causality sow,
grow a possible branch of time,
eight worlds wide,
best enjoy the ride,
todays the day
and
the hours mine.

TOM B.

Life *(Composed 1997)*

Life is a wonderful thing,
The glory of trees in the spring,
The days, the months, the years,
The happiness, the tears.

For the pain we have to bear,
God is always there -
He shows us his love in so many ways,
When the shadows fall, on our darkest days,
That is when we know we need Him there,
He listens to our every prayer.

Thank you, God, for your beautiful world,
For the earth, the sky, the sea,
For loved ones, for people everywhere
And for the life you have given to me.

VERA ANNIE WEBB…NÉE WAY…

Summer Thoughts *(Composed 2002)*

On a Summer's day…

A little bird, he sings his melody,
- A sound so sweet –
To tell his joy of life to me,
And yet how short is life,
How brief our stay…
We dare not waste
A single day,
But hold these hours close to our heart
And cherish them.
Give love, and gentleness impart.

Sing a sweet song…

           until we say goodnight,

We loved it all!

VERA ANNIE WEBB…NÉE WAY…

Space and Nature

Morning Awakes *(Composed 1975)*

- For my Grandfather -

A gust of breeze stirs the trees
And sunlight shines, in narrow lines,
Amidst the clouds, cold and grey,
Sending forth an orange ray…

Melting mist and morning frost,
Translucent scenes to all are tossed –
A message meant for everyone,
Dull night is drowned by morning sun.

ANNETTE-FRANCES B.

Forgotten *(Composed 1975)*

Swans - noble, elegant and serene.
Willow trees swaying. Envisage the scene.
Peace and solitude, gifts from the lake,
Endless paths around to take.

Wandering pathways, shrouded in trees,
Wind around hills and end in these:
Streets of uneven paving stones,
Blessed with litter and traffic zones.
Edged with houses, derelict and old.
Always for sale, but never sold.

ANNETTE-FRANCES B.

Favourite Place *(Composed 1974)*

The powerful, eternal waves,
Jagged rocks and dark caves,
Seagulls circling in the sky,
Uttering their eery, haunting cry,
The sun's golden rainbows, mingling with the sea,
This deserted beach, the perfect haunt for me.

ANNETTE-FRANCES B.

Little Bird *(Composed 1995)*

There he lives his little life,
Midst the trees, the leaves, the rain,
There he sings his song so fine,
And he fills this heart of mine.

There is hope and joy and peace,
There is God above, I know,
Looking down with caring face,
Giving all his creatures grace.

Little bird, you know it's true,
He loves us still, and he loves you.
You are happy all your days,
Through clouds and sun, you sing his praise.

VERA ANNIE WEBB…NÉE WAY…

Sights and Sounds I Love *(Composed 1995)*

Blackbird there upon the post,
Songs like yours I love the most,
Birds and flowers, all of these,
And the music in the trees.
There is movement in the sky,
When the wind is rushing by,
There is rhythm in the earth,
When the spring is giving birth.
There are birdsongs on the hill,
In the Summer evening still.

Windmills white, gentle breeze,
Dreamy downs, buzzing bees,
Craggy cliffs, proud and high,
Fields so green, sapphire sky,
Crying, gliding gulls in flight,
Dusk falls then creatures of the night,
Once more, their mystery trails pursue,
'till, later, breaks the dawning new!

VERA ANNIE WEBB...NÉE WAY...

Dandelions and Buttercups *(Composed 1997)*

Little wildflowers, golden, bright,
Sprinkled on the bank so high,
When the wind your seeds has blown,
Faraway again you roam.

No one puts you into pots,
Nor plants you in a fine display,
Freedom is your happy lot,
As you weave your merry way.

Sometimes you are trodden down,
Or pulled, or cut, and lose your crown!
But still you wander somewhere new,
To glow again your colour true.

You are humble, just a weed,
In wild places, there you lead,
He knows you well, he made you bright,
Little flowers of God's delight.

VERA ANNIE WEBB…NÉE WAY…

Winter Scene *(Composed 2004)*

From my window…

So still the trees,
Reaching to the winter sky
Thin branches, dark are these,
Bare and dark and still…
No breeze has come to stir the trees,
Nor stir the holly on the hill.

Is it a picture in a frame?
Is this a dream in silhouette?
The movement of life has ceased,
As if a spell was cast, and yet…
All will return, the rhythm, the sound,
The wild wind howling all around,
Birds clinging to branches as they sway,
Clinging and singing their joy,
All giving and living life's day.

VERA ANNIE WEBB…NÉE WAY…

What If? *(Composed 2020)*

Mercury is slightly appealing,
its misty, mystic and magical appearance
but what would we meet?
Aliens with long,
green and purple tentacles,
scarlet menacing eyes,
long banana fingers,
and chocolate dipped fingernails?

I've just discovered that Venus is named after
a Roman God of love and beauty.
Ai, my name, means love and indigo blue, in Japanese.
What if there were dragons,
hiding amongst the Venus volcanoes,
waiting to spring up?
What if dragons are
hidden in the core of the earth?

The red spot of Jupiter is an eye,
the eye of Jupiter,
like a dragon's realm and a swirling storm.
Jupiter is occupied by a black hole,
a place where even light cannot escape.
Where does all this light go?
Or is the black hole just a mystic, moon shadow?

Uranus is a wonderful blue,
as blue as the sea.
Why is it lopsided?
Perhaps it crashed into its twin planet, Neptune,
perhaps that made it lopsided.
Why has it got so many rings? Why is it lopsided?

Neptune is an amazing twin to Uranus,
its wonders are everlasting,
endless,
its colour a deep blue of wonder.

Did you know Mars is named after the Roman God of war?
Mars is a rusty,
oxidized iron or coppery colour.

Saturn is another amazing planet.
Is there anything on it?
Maybe dragons, of ice and fire,
slide down the wonderful,
colossal rings of Saturn.
The seven rings are magnificent, marvellous slides.

As we whizz by,
to the end of the universe,
a journey of everlasting adventure.

A. D. BRANNON (age 8)

Still Moving I Sat *(Composed 2003)*

Still moving, I sat,
watching a single leaf fall from a tree.
A hundred million people passed me by,
taillights, like rockets,
headlights, like eyes.
All in but a moment,
things born,
cry,
shout,
laugh,
die.
And round it goes.
The world spins another thousand times,
hurtling around the sun,
burning through galaxies,
like pin head whirlpools,
dancing the waltz
in the infinite lake of space.

It is all energy, movement and change,
flowing along the tracks of time.
Nothing ever stands still,
but how can we see anything,
when nothing rests?
Everything is a blur,
like living in white light.

Purity doesn't exist,
it's just a paradoxical ideal.

Everything is connected,
things don't just cease to be,
consisting of only one thing in isolation.
In fact, there are no edges,
the colours all blend,
change is a graduated movement,
from one momentary conscious recognition
to the next.
The only true security with definition,
is by accepting what has been allowed to happen.
We have no control,
just recognition.

Things are what they are, for a reason.
To question is to hold out your fingers,
like brakes,
dragging behind you,
until you wear them down to the bone
and still you keep moving.

ALEX LOUIS WAY BRANNON

Peace not War...

Why? *(Composed year 2003)*

There are jewels, of every colour, in the blink of every eye.
There is sweet perfume, from every smell,
in the draw of every breath.
There are love stories, from the song of every bird,
in the moment of every word.
There is nectar, from every honey, in the taste of every bite
and
there is softness, from every rose,
in the exchange of every touch.

The world is as rich as our imagination,
a great show of eternal love…

So why,
why do we have money within our eyes,
success in our nostrils,
anger in our ears,
bitterness in our mouths,
and guns in
our
hands
?

ALEX LOUIS WAY BRANNON

Song *(Composed 1995)*

- Let's find love -

Let's find love,
Start at the beginning,
We are one,
The human race.

Let's forget,
The losing or the winning,
We all win
And we find God's grace

Grace is strength,
Helping one another,
No more greed,
Then we find joy.

Let's find joy…
Find the joy in living,
As one world and family.

Now…

Let's find love.

VERA ANNIE WEBB…NÉE WAY…

Look Into the Eyes of Humanity
(Composed 2008)

The truth is there, look into their eyes…
What do we see in these human eyes?
Are they happy or sad, are they good, or bad?
The truth is there, look into their eyes…

Are they the passengers of their thought and action –
to complete, from when they are born to when they die?
Their satisfaction, while others raise arms and cry?
What have humans done to this planet?
Is there no end to this self-destruction,
this careless corruption?

Is there an assumption that they own this earth?
They don't, they are wrong…
We are nothing but guests, from birth, until we are gone.
Is there light at the end of their plastic tunnel of pollution?
Do they have a solution or are we in deepest trouble?

The truth is there, look into their eyes…

R. W. BRANNON

General War *(Composed in the late 1950's / 1960's)*

Not to the nations who would fight to defend, but to the 'would be aggressor'

A fictitious man, though he's 'carried the can,'
and he's carried it since the world began.
He gives his name to one and all,
and bids us follow at his call,
but youth, you know his cunning tricks,
to allure you when he'd thinks it fit.
His name is known to all before,
none other than, old 'General War.'
He calls to young and old alike,
"Come, join me in this glorious fight."
He's cunning, ever on the watch,
more so when markets pile with stocks,
for then supplies do head demand,
this is disastrous, understand?
Old General War says, "Now's the chance,
I'll use my power again, announce,
to all the people truly loyal,
to come and join me in this toil."
Let's all unite as fathers did
and draw the sword again, to bid,
that young and old may march again
and plunder in this 'so called fame.'
When will our nations learn?
Perhaps again too late, in turn
to bear upon their shoulders more,
again, the tyranny of war.
What means it in a world of scorn,
that makes the widows, mothers, mourn?

And in the past, when guns have thundered,
it's very sure, someone has blundered,
far better then, to make peace stable,
to settle debts around a table.
Perchance had this been done, in days gone by,
our folk would never 've had to die
in such unholy circumstance,
and it would give the world a better chance
to so develop, for mankind,
those things which we have left behind.
Will the nations learn a lesson,
now that General War is guessing?
For the past that brought him glory,
now, seems to tell another story.
Hydrogen and atom now,
could fit the general and allow
more disaster on this earth,
not to his benefit or mirth,
'Says he' "This is not a fake
that is holding me at stake."
Tis a weapon of destruction,
maybe like volcán eruption
 - mankind who presented it, scientist and 'clever wit' -
what price glory be it said, this bomb may also heal, instead?
Now perhaps his warriors think more wise
and fail to listen to his cries.
Says the general, 'once supreme' -
"Now, all my efforts seem a dream."
What if the nations join as one
and do as God's: "...will be done" ?
A victory to us be sure,
e'en though it's never been before.

So let's all say, this fiction man,
no more may need to 'bear the can' -
no more, that man may heed to hate,
for General War is out of date.
Don't let us ever slam the door
and be a slave to General War,
who knows, the bomb may be humane,
not to be used in war again.
To even say, we have the answer –
perhaps, maybe, to cure the cancer.

Griffin E. D. Way

A minor change has been made, to one line on page 28. Originally a quotation was included, from a famous and very beautiful folk song, but the process to secure permission, to quote and acknowledge one line, was likely to be time consuming; hence it was removed and replaced.

We Cannot Change the World *(Composed 1994)*

Long ago, I really thought it could be done,
We could change the world and build a perfect one,
Every land would live in peace,
All the bitterness would cease,
It was just a happy dream, when I was young.

But now I know the truth is not the same,
For many men still play their cruel game,
They will not learn, they cannot tell,
That they are only building hell
Upon this earth, so beautiful to claim.

VERA ANNIE WEBB…NÉE WAY…

People *(Composed 1995)*

All the people in the world
Are just like you and me,
Men and women, hand in hand,
Wanting to be free,
But there are marches, there are uniforms,
And men still grasp a gun,
Why can't we leave them far behind?
Then all of us have won!

We'll find the joy in life again!
Help each other, rich and poor,
Share our dreams and share our pain,
Understand each other more.
Leave the shadows, see the light!
We're one great family!
For all the people in the world
Are just like you and me.

VERA ANNIE WEBB…NÉE WAY…

(Musical Lyrics composed 2019)

Betrayer's Voice

YOU GOTTA SHOOT THE DICE
YOU GOTTA SHAKE THE BET
DON'T MOURN YOUR LIFE
CAUSE IT AINT DONE YET

I GOTTA THAW MY TRY
MOVE OUT THE DOOR
WHERE'S THE MAP N THE WHY
I SET FIRE TO THE FLOOR

NOW LET'S GO

DON'T ASK ME WHERE

JUST LET'S GO

I AM SO PAST THE CARE

AND F***ING GO

Defy the street, the road and grass
Defy the way things come to pass
The day of reasons on its ass
Now all we have to do is last.

So, what's succinct I think just sunk
We need to sync, rethink, debunk
In reach of all, in breach of none,
Each thought like waiting shaolin monks

>Solos start.<
Warped.-WHAT DO WE… KNOW?-
>DRUMS<
>SOLOS CULMINATION<
>Solos back2riff<

YOU GOTTA SHOOT THE DICE
YOU GOTTA SHAKE THE BET
DON'T MOURN YOUR LIFE
CAUSE IT AINT DONE YET

I GOTTA THAW MY TRY
MOVE OUT THE DOOR
WHERE'S THE MAP N THE WHY
I SET FIRE TO THE FLOOR

NOW LET'S GO

DON'T ASK ME WHERE

JUST LET'S GO

I AM SO PAST THE CARE

LEEEEEEEEEETS GO!!

My coins are the betrayers voice
Slide into quickened amble
They have me and I have no choice
But their machine's a ceaseless gamble

Shake your head like your thought fell out
End aint dead if you go around
So why exist frozen in doubt
Let's spend incendiary rounds

(Echo) Go go go go…
\>DRUMS/LEAD GIUTAR<

Highjack a metaphor
Buy back the real before
Sigh, then you fight the war
Freedoms cost be all the more

Drum/bass led solo.

Defy the street, the road and grass
Defy the way things come to pass
The day of reasons on its ass
Now all we have to do is last

So, what's succinct I think just sunk
We need to sync, rethink, debunk
In reach of all, in breach of none
Each thought like waiting shaolin monks

\>solos culmination<

- No don't let go-
-Yeah lets go!!!!-

TOM B.

(Musical lyrics composed 2001)

THERMO NUCLEAR TWISTER

Raging banshee wail of survival
Riot to the race of the pace of your rival
Is it moving too fast?
Another day hit your past
Are you jumping round the outside
Swinging, kicking off the trees or
Stuck inside the fear of fear
With the grass stains on your knees?
Somebody somewhere never went anywhere.
Nobody everywhere everybody run!! (STOPS)

A voodoo ball this ether'l* plain
The pins fell out, but the holes remain
What? Can't we f***ing start again
How much for that planet and a new f***ing brain?

Woke from a world I created in a dream
To this conscious expectant calculation of machine
Vote for the panic of the moral of the day
Never understanding, standing under what you say

Some gasoline a loaf of bread
Some holy deeds were made with lead
A thought a means a speech of dread
Cross trampolines inside my head

Now face is green
Spin right to red
The turn has been
The word is spread

Er, paper heads control for less
Radio sire, wire servo mesh
Steal prosthesis in evening dress
A kamikaze pastry chef

Now face is green
Roll right to red
The turn has been
Re roll they said

Raging banshee wail of survival
Riot to the race of the pace of your rival
Is it moving too fast?
Another day hit your past
Are you jumping round the outside
Swinging, kicking off the trees or
Stuck inside the fear of fear
With the grass stains on your knees….
Somebody somewhere never went anywhere.
Nobody everywhere everybody run!! (STOPS)

A voodoo ball this ether'l plain
The pins fell out, but the holes remain
What? Can't we f***ing start again
How much for that planet and a new f***ing brain?

Woke from a world I created in a dream
To this conscious expectant calculation of machine
Vote for the panic of the moral of the day
Never understanding standing under what you say

Limbs entwine contort in fright
More to the power of the hate of their plight
Behold the darkness burns so bright
We told you suckers to stand and fight

Now face is green
Roll right to red
The turn has been
and all are dead.

TOM B.

*Ether'l - ethereal

Nuclear Weapons – War... *(Composed 1976)*

What have you done to my world,
The sun, the air and sea?
What have you done to my world,
And what has happened to me?

Now there is darkness and dust,
Once, there were fields and flowers.
Now, there is no time,
Once, a day held many hours.

Oh, why did you kill our world?
Who granted you this power?
And, how do you feel right now,
In this your victory hour?

Now, a child cannot learn
Of love and life on earth.
Now, the earth is cold,
There will be no birth.

Oh, what have you done to my world,
The sun, the air and sea?
Oh, what have you done to my world,
And what has happened to me?

ANNETTE-FRANCES B.

I Think About the World *(Composed 1986)*

I think about the world,
Its cruelty and its sadness all around,
I think about the world,
And wonder why contentment can't be found.
The darkened places, the frightened faces
Of the people who should live in peace.
The countries fighting and children dying.
When will it ever cease?

There are so many things,
That could fill our lives with joy and light,
The world has much to share,
If we could only see the beauty, bright.
I think about the world,
And though I cannot really understand,
I feel someday, somehow,
That peace, and love 'will' shine in every land.

VERA ANNIE WEBB…NÉE WAY…

Freedom or Oppression?

(Musical lyrics 2017)

Welcome to the GAHC!

<u>Chorus</u> Suit keeps face where a smile is placed.
If you can't make peace
make up make haste

recruit distaste, where guile disgraced
if our pain increase
wake up, take place.

-

Oblique you speak and power leak
so, everybody takes a seat
yet every time that ends might meet
you tie our laces feet to feet

people are your underfoot
you balance your position
disciple pawn another rook
grand a**hole competition.

-

<u>Chorus</u>

-

So, talk is fine, how much who knows
your t's and i's are swords and bows
so walk this line. See trees of crows.
How many died do you suppose?

Your minds been eaten by your pride
unkind and blind, you cash sweet lies
your truth your plight another rigged fight.
Peace and quiet, though no one sleeps tight.

<u>Chorus</u>

The poison trade left dead on boarders
chicken flavour trachea disorder
brains and guts disease gets broader
supermarket zombie hoarder,

mistrust sawdust bloody its mix
when the goal retreats the game is fixed.
Your medicine is rhetoric
if that's the cure I am better sick.

<u>Chorus</u>

Belief so strong it kills the concept
right cast wrong let's make an omelette
crushed n gone tall tale looms onset
what was '1' betrays the context.

Yes love is our equality.
Brother do I owe apologies
for purging these minorities
self rectitude anthology.

Suit keeps face where a smile is placed.
If you can't make peace
make up make haste

recruit distaste, where guile disgraced
if our pain increase
wake up, take place.

Oblique you speak and power leak
so everybody takes a seat
yet every time that ends might meet
you tie our laces feet to feet

people are your underfoot
you balance your position
disciple pawn another rook
grand a**hole competition.

Your worth is net
but sos regret
our bleeding guts
your next project.

TOM B.

(Chorus from the musical lyrics composed 1998)

Cliché

CHORUS 1:

And so, you've heard it all before
Another song you can ignore
These labels that we carry on
In separation we go wrong
With social fronts we're forced to don
We've held our thoughts in for too long…

TOM B.

Hypocrite Boogie

(Composed 2012)

The story of a child
With eyes so wild
The love inside could not be filed
He lived to feel
And could not conceal
His longing for a better deal
He cried
He'd hide
He never lied
Until the day his brain defied
Was pushed and pulled a twisted turn
It was then his mind began to burn
For vengeance now this man did yearn
So, on the program he did turn
And these are the sounds he made:
I don't have the reasons, you don't have the rhyme
So, let's all take it easy and fake another time
We can't live in fear or doped up on our hope
Now sink another beer, just to help you cope.
Let's run around the garden screaming murder in our ears
Don't tell me I'm a hypocrite or this will end in tears
I love this place but hate the taste
I wish we could be clear
But till we wake up from our schemes
the end will not be near
You make me laugh
You make me cry
You make me live and die
You try to make me change my mind
but that won't ever fly

These tears are real
This pain I feel
I love you, don't despair,
But when it comes right down to it
I really couldn't care!
xxx

S. A. W. BRANNON

Omega *(Composed 2013)*

So,
this is it – this great abyss.
This chasm - where once there was
pride,
achievement,
happiness,
success.

Fools,
idiots,
b-----ds!
Why did they kill the soul that led them?
The spirit,
the music,
the creativity.

They
entrusted us with precious cargo.
We nurtured,
educated,
listened,
understood,
cared.

They,
with their acrylic designer nails,
extended hair,
false bodies,
dull brains,
idol gossip
and
minuscule minds,
chose
murder,
destruction,
annihilation,
extermination,
eradication.

They,
within their insular, pseudo world,
destroyed the living, breathing spirit of
creativity,
kindness,
humanity
and hope.

Why
then are they still
free,
happy
and successful

within their painted, plastic tombs?
Whilst those who once understood
and led humanity are devoid of life?

Why
?

ANNETTE-FRANCES B.

Fleeting Glimpse – Port of Calais, Summer 2015*

Angry faces –
Seeking utopia in a hostile mechanical city.
Sultry space – monstrous wheels – oppressive gangs,
relinquishing poverty – opposing politics – 'fighting the fight' –
Possible justification? Safe-haven – ultimate unity,
pledge of freedom or 'a free ride'?

Young mother –
Clammy face – deep lines etched by the burden of uncertainty.
Tired limbs - worn mind - still tongue,
entrapped by the silence of inconceivable fears.

Young child (girl about 8)
Moist face - exhausted by the phantom of insecurity.
Limp hair - fragile body - still tongue.
Wild eyes filled with unshed tears.

Mother and child –
Hand in hand, seeking freedom in a hostile mechanical city.
Searching – waiting – planning.
Deep love – faint hope – silent objective.
Justification? Plea for humanity – citizenship –
liberty – autonomy.

ANNETTE-FRANCES B.

*In 2015, during a strike at the Port of Calais, numerous migrants tried boarding lorries - all were searching for places beneath or within each lorry, in order to enter England. Inadvertently, we witnessed this occurrence, whilst in our family car, queuing in a lane intended for lorries.

Survival of the Fittest *(Composed 2003)*

Money holds no respect here,
only what it can buy…
Respect, status,
they're not about knowledge, or work,
they're about strength.
Basic, primeval strength,
how hard you can hit,
how much you can take,
who has the most back up and…
how far they are willing to go to honour you,
how sharp your blade is,
how fast your car is…
How many laws can you break, get away with and laugh about?
How many times can you get knocked down,
still get up and scrabble to the top,
to prove your respect and reinstall the momentary fear?

It's all a measure to define physical boundaries,
from one man to the next.
Respect, a side effect, derived from the pain and fear.
A momentary, pseudo adequacy,
until the next measure.

He hides himself away, so he can be like the next,
who's like the next…who's like the next…
And so, it continues, into one big circle of inhuman, numbness.
He sits in a darkened room,

       on his own,

              licking his wounds, from the day's work.

As the sun sets, for a moment, a hope rises in his mind.
A few echoing words, come from deep inside,
a dream of getting out…
He dreams of a house with a garden,
away from the violence,
a place where he can be himself,
a place, where he has a wife and children to love
and to love him.
He can talk to people and they respect him,
for things other than the reinforcing of his own reputation,
but the harsh reality, of his world,
cuts through like a blade…
The worry comes back,
the fear of the inevitability,
that tomorrow someone bigger will come,
knock from him his measure, of fearful respect,
knock him back into the gutter,
in a pool of beaten blood…

When the sun goes down,
they all dream for a moment.
They're all trapped in a circle of fear,
locked within a cycle of fear.
Embrace the gutter.
Be the "weakest" –
It's the way out.
It's the realisation, of you.

ALEX LOUIS WAY BRANNON

Work and Routine

The Manager Saves the Day *(Composed 2011)*

A proud young manager, named Jay,
attended a special first aid training-day.
At staunching blood and CPR,
he soon became a perfect star.

With glossy certificate safely attained,
pride demanded that it be framed,
in solid Canadian maple wood,
and hung in a place where the light was good.

He screwed the screw tight in the wall,
hoping that it wouldn't fall.
Alas it fell down on the head,
of an aged volunteer called Fred.

Fred groaned "It was deliberate - I just know.
You're a dangerous manager. You must go.
Look I'm bleeding - all over the place.
There's a cut on my head and a cut on my face."

"Keep calm," called Jay, "I've just been trained,
in treatment of the sick and maimed.
I know exactly what to do.
You should be pleased I'm here with you."

ANNETTE-FRANCES B.

Always Purchase Your Car Tax on Time
(Composed 2011)

(Based on the good old days when one could drive around,
with a 'tax applied for' disc on the car window!)

I soaked my feet, then brushed my hair
and settled in my comfy chair,
with T.V., coffee and a chocolate bar,
to view a film, with my favourite star.
Suddenly in you burst, in a fearful panic,
facial expression totally manic.

You really were in a terrible state,
as you uttered these words, at a rapid rate:
"The police saw my car, with no tax in view.
I need cash quick, so I can renew -
the disc, right now and avoid a fine -
so, I'm selling the T.V. don't start to whine."

As you whisked it away, before my eyes,
impervious to my shouts and cries,
a neighbour peered, cautiously, around her curtain,
uttering disparaging whispers, you can be certain.
I followed you - with no shoes on my feet,
and shouted insults, right out in the street:

"Your engine is hanging by a wire.
It's burning oil. It may catch fire.
It shrieks and leaks, at each twist and turn.
You paid too much. When will you learn?"
"Don't worry," you called, "I'll be back quite soon,
I'll borrow a telly, you'll be over the moon."

You returned with a tax disc and two old T.V. sets.
"Will they work? What's the bets."
One actually worked - well just the sound.
You placed it carefully, on the ground.
The other, its audio totally dead,
managed some visual scenes instead.

Hence, to tackle the task of fine tuning,
really was quite time consuming -
until I discovered it was much more fun
to view a ballet, on channel one,
whilst relaxing with a cup of tea,
engrossed in the murder on channel three.

ANNETTE-FRANCES B.

Vicious Cycle *(Musical lyrics composed 2005)*

AKA a metal rock ode to a washing machine.

BEAT DOWN REVOLUTIONS OF THE DRUM
SPIN OUT NOT ALL IS SAID AND DONE
Brain-tain fractal react
Main frame anti matter fact
BREAK OUT REVOLUTIONS OF THE DRUM
NO DOUBT GIVE THE BERSERK BEAT SOME

Separate, iron face down
Light n dark goes round and round
These serotonin stains are drowned
A coin a slot no out of bounds

Synthetic dye in clean regret
A tie caught in your temper set
360 degrees heated wet
Load, spin, wait, beep lest you forget

Fabric softener pineal gland
An eco rinse this sudding land
Reload machine rolls under hand
Pillow for your thoughts like contraband

BEAT DOWN REVOLUTIONS OF THE DRUM
SPIN OUT NOT ALL IS SAID AND DONE
Brain-tain fractal react or!??
Main frame anti matter fact er?
BREAK OUT REVOLUTIONS OF THE DRUM
NO DOUBT GIVE THE BERSERK BEAT SOME

I just can't wait to see this box
My centrifugal stripy socks
A cattle prod of static shocks
A rev-o-lute dye paradox?

Bleach wore down my hypothalam's*
The colours run, wear indistinct,
I am not sure where my shirt begins
The cycles done and I got lint

Today I load up rod concrete
And busted coins to make a beat
A cyclone drum knocks trench through street
It got the mustard off my sheets

BEAT DOWN REVOLUTIONS OF THE DRUM
SPIN OUT NOT ALL IS SAID AND DONE
Brain-tain fractal reactor**
Main frame anti matter factor
BREAK OUT REVOLUTIONS OF THE DRUM
NO DOUBT GIVE THE BERSERK BEAT SOME

TOM B.

*hypothalam's (hypothalamus) – part of the brain, with small nuclei, one role of the nuclei involves linking the nervous system to the endocrine system (via the pituitary gland). The endocrine system controls many things, including 'sleep and mood'.

** fractal reactor – a form of nuclear power

(Musical Lyrics Composed 2014)

X Directional Hard Work

If I cast my thoughts asunder
how many try and steal my thunder?
Defeat myself with senseless wonder,
retreat into a future tundra.

Sit a while and look for faces,
sell my smile to empty spaces,
stack a pile, uncharted places
twist the dial and burn the aces.

A state of mind
a martial state
don't feel inclined
emancipate
if you rewind
don't integrate
release the grind
and try fly straight
-
straight through them
straight for you
spiral through it
arrive anew.

Pre-set the stereotype disdain,
exempt from every social reign,
the expectation leading bane
contempt into the sight ingrain.

Pry tooth-ed slug off weathered skull
and play life's theme, bugged head of holes,
defuse the plug, shot light so dull,
if words could shrug, they'd steal the show.

The trap is sprung
but missed the meat
the road winds on
you hit the street
kick start, ride on,
block, flow and leap
contours bruise strong
strike gates, fly straight
-
hate from them
straight to you
create, destroy
now what to do.

A canvas man as time draws on
a sandwich van the picnics gone.
Horizon endless road forlorn
and on the wall the petrol runs.

Two points to find a line between
blink strobe spotlights leave polka'd scheme
amongst the field the moles have been
or join the clots adrenaline.

A state of mind
a martial state
don't feel inclined
emancipate
if you rewind
don't integrate
release the grind
fly straight fly straight

irate again
so, wait for who?
Spiral through 'em,
let them eat shoe.

So, strike a pose until it dies,
shuffle your toes straight off a high rise,
go lone, morose is in disguise,
stare at your nose for invisible flies.

Dust and mysteries, stories built
busted histories lock each floor,
solemn the breeze, but rumbling silt
Golem breathes through opened door.

You're not undone
know no defeat
the road winds on
you hit the street
swing a pylon
shock those you beat
take a style on,
crush gates, fly straight
-
Straight through them
take the view
my proxy block,
may step on you.

TOM B.

Supermarket Chaos *(Composed 2014)*

Shopping with Parkinson's disease can cause chaos at times…

'Freezing' -
this is a good one to
annoy people.
It's easy,
just put an imaginary goldfish bowl over your head,
wait for someone to talk to you…
Within a split second, your mind freezes,
you see, you hear, you do not process…

Here's another little ditty:
now enter your local supermarket,
ensure it's at its busiest time,
perhaps just after schools have closed,
to achieve full benefit and cause most chaos.
Take a trolley – to aid your balance.
Struggle precariously through aisles,
in slow, but reckless fashion.
People will scatter in panic,
as you bump and crash your way through.

Now,
laboriously wheel your five items to the checkout,
making sure you form
the front of a long queue,
whilst you have on your miserable,
mask like face –
hypomimia* at its best.
Fumble your bank card,
from your wallet.

Now,
while shaking,
attempt to put the card in the slot,
don't forget to...

                                                take your time...

because you have 'all day' – right?
The more you tell your hand to stop shaking,
it will do the opposite,
especially as you go to punch your number in,
and as you try to avoid tapping the silly shield
that covers half the machine.

Try -
try again.
Damn!
You've pressed the wrong number.
By now, the people behind you
are p—d off
and are moving their stuff
to the next till
or
spitting nasty comments.
This is usually well past the 'tutting' stage
and past the stage where a little boy
is asking:
"Mummy, why is that man shaking?"

Finally, when you've managed to pay,
go outside,
put your five items in your car,
take your trolley,
push the chain in.

Can you get your token out?
No?
Try again, slowly.
Oh no!
Now, you have an added 'bonus' –
you are upsetting people
who wanted a trolley - Ha! Ha!

When you arrive home,
your wife will ask,
"Why were you so long?"

R. W. BRANNON

*Hypomimia – Face, with virtually no facial expression, like a blank mask. The muscles can cause this to occur with Parkinson's.

Resolutions *(Composed 2017)*

When we try to make these things,
we often try in vain.

We promise this and promise that,
no matter what the pain.

We hope to keep them,
that is true.

I know it's hard
and so, do you.

There are better ways,
or so they say.

Perhaps there are,
please show the way.

I often have good intentions,
they always seem so fine.

Are they just pretentions?
Maybe: but they're in time.

When others fail,
I pity them.

I do not laugh.
I don't condemn.

If they should succeed,
I then feel good.

I say Godspeed.
Or so I should!

So, let us all,
in this New Year,

try not to fall,
or live in fear.

Let's all walk tall:
let us be kind.

Fit body now -
in clear fit mind.

DAVID KING

Inventions *(Composed 2012)*

I often seem to invent things by accident:
things which are no use at all.
I recently invented...
a knot making machine in my kitchen drawer.
You can have one too.
Just drop a few of your phone charger wires in
and close the drawer.

In order to make the knots,
wait till you need a charger in a hurry.

Simply pull out the required charger wire
and you will discover a very complicated and original knot.
You can make it permanent
 if you become impatient and pull, then shake it.
This knot is so original that it defies undoing
and you will have to drag out the unwanted charger wires,
along with the one you want.

It's the same with wire coat hangers,
- Oh yes, we all know they breed in the secret of darkness -
You reach in and simply select the one you want,
you know: the pink one for your in-fashion dress.
It may come out,
but two others will come out with it,
trailing everything you don't want.

The automatic mustard spoon finder is in my kitchen drawer.
This tiny and little used spoon sits with six,
man sized teaspoons.
It will always come out if you dare to feel for a real spoon,
one which can scoop up a hot tea bag and
'not' drop it on your bare foot.
I want to patent this automatic mustard spoon finder.

DAVID KING

Paradox *(Composed 2012)*

Paradox…
What is it?
To explain, we may consult a dictionary
and it may tell us it is a statement that may
look ridiculous, but perhaps 'may' be true…

Escher did it this way: He simply drew a lone pipe…
and wrote underneath that it 'wasn't' a pipe.
He wrote this in French.
He made many impossible shapes
and the most famous may be:
the triangle with three right angles.
In reality this could only make three sides
which can never meet.

Gödel did the same with numbers,
which are beyond me to explain.
J. S. Bach composed paradoxical fugues
I can hear, but not explain.

Science fiction gives us many strange situations,
including time travel, which transports us into the past.
We are then posed with the choice of an action,
which would negate our very existence.

Random numbers,
which seem to have no relevance,
can be seen to add up -
in any direction.
With an odd number magic square there is a very simple
and logical progression:
it 'can' be explained.
With an even number magic square,
it takes many complex calculations to explain.

Surely, we can survive 'without' absolutes
because near approximates are enough.
Nothing is ever what it seems,
because if this were so
then we COULD have a triangle with three right angles!
Ask Escher!

DAVID KING

As Morning Tones *(Composed 2005)*

As morning tones
there are moans and groans,
sticks and stones,
aching bones
and the melodic drones
of mobile phones.

There are a thousand eyes
of salary guys,
souls in disguise,
of shirts and ties,
awaiting the prize
of a train to arise.

All standing in line,
all prisoners of time,
seven till nine,
sifting the grime
and watching the sign.

Exchanging stares,
from their office chairs,
while they count the stocks
and they count the shares
of countless affairs
and all of it tears,
because someone cares.

Once so bold,
their lives unfold
from young to old,
with eyes so cold
in days untold.
All for the price of a little gold.
All for the fear of breaking the mould.

ALEX LOUIS WAY BRANNON

First Flat – Somewhere in Muswell Hill
(Composed 1978)

Just a tumble-down flat, with an outside loo,
no hot water, yet worries were few.
Wallpaper peeling. Floor so bare,
but life was fun when we lived there!

Just large hollow rooms, with high ceilings and draft,
in need of good decor and handicraft.
Furniture old, patched and worn.
Garden a jungle, overgrown lawn.

But neighbours were good, family were too,
and as we lived there, a homeliness grew.
Our cat gave us kittens. We were never alone,
in that tumble-down flat, we called our home.

ANNETTE-FRANCES B.

Relationships...

Parted *(Composed 1999)*

We did not know,
Blindly we did not see…
        One day…
The story would be told.
We thought the chapters
Would go on,
New days ever to unfold.
But now the door to yesterday
        Is shut,
And oh, so tight.
You are beyond that door,
And I am here,
In often lonely day,
And always lonely night.

But I can see you there,
In the old days that we knew,
Through the mists of memory,
I am still with you.

VERA ANNIE WEBB…NÉE WAY

Poetical Reflections *(Composed 2012)*

Well, did Kipling say it all?
In his poem *If* he could have said:
"Then you'll be a woman, my daughter!"
 But then, it would not flow so well...

Thomas Gray's *Elegy in a Country Churchyard*
Seems to catch me more,
With the powerful line:
"Full many a flower is born to blush unseen."

Andrew Marvell's *To his Coy Mistress* excites me,
He ventures all the way in his love for her, when he writes:
 "Thus, though we cannot make our sun
  Stand still, yet we will make him run."

"Two souls with but a single thought,
 Two hearts that beat as one" - Keats was well ahead of time,
Some modern science now shows us that two people,
In a state of complete empathy,
'Can' cause their hearts to synchronise.

Elizabeth Barrett Browning demonstrates
Truly three-dimensional love when she says:
"I love thee to the depth and breadth and height
 My soul can reach..."

So many of these great poets have gone all the way for love.
William Shakespeare writes in *Sonnet XVIII*:
"So long as men can breathe or eyes can see,
 So long lives this, and this gives life to thee."
And in *Twelfth Night* - he writes so musically:
"Trip no further, pretty sweeting,
 Journeys end in lovers meeting."

I finish with a lighter journey - Edward Lear's
  - *The Owl and the Pussy-Cat* -
"They sailed away, for a year and a day,
  To the land where the bong tree grows."

DAVID KING

My One and Only Vera *(Composed 2019)*

Of all the things I love about you,
Here's a few among the many.
Whatever you said, I always found true,
Of untrue: there never were any.

You brightened up every day of my life.
You are the brightest star I've ever known.
I wish I could have made you my wife.
I wish I could have made you my own.

Your smile and your beauty always filled me with joy,
Your kindness, your love and your care,
This happiness made us feel, like a girl and a boy,
It made us go, wherever we dare.

So, let us keep flying and loving and more
And let us keep doing our thing,
For the love that you gave goes right to my core,
So, let us just sing, sing, sing.

DAVID KING

Nobody in the World
(Composed 2006)

Nobody in the world will ever make me
feel the way you do.
You put a smile on my face, whenever
you are near me,
your cuddles and kisses send me
to heaven.
The look in your eyes gives me that
tingly feeling
that I never want to go away.

The only thing I want you to know
- and believe it, 'cause it's true -
you're everything I want
and I'm so in love with you!

L. A. BRANNON

Toast to Our Love
(Composed 1979)

Oh, what love I have for the woman in my life,
as she seems to draw my heart like a magnet
and my soul, with hers, into infinity –
and so, this is for you my darling,
and for our dreams, everlasting and companionship.

R. W. BRANNON

If I Lived a Million Times
(Composed 2013)

You amaze me
Then appraise me
Sometimes our love it starts to phase me
But every day you re-engage me
I never want to lose you baby.

So, if I lived a million times
To cultivate a billion rhymes
I'd live again, suffer any pain
To bring you back to love again.

I'm sorry if I call your bluff
But sometimes this life is just too tough
And yet you stand there in the rough
Shining through, more than enough
And yes, I wrote this off the cuff
So, you know it's true
I love you Lu.

S. A. W. BRANNON

To my Father *(Composed: 2000)*

- Farewell -

Young hands, resting on old hands,
stretched across the years.
Young life, watching old life,
through the curtain of life's fears.

Amidst this ancient mist,
mind's muddled end is near.
I call you 'Dad' - just one more time
and suddenly you hear.

Clarity's captured for a second
and I can see you understand,
for you call me 'little sweetheart'
and you squeeze my hand.

ANNETTE FRANCES B.

Do you Like Italian Opera? *(Composed 2014)*

To my Uncle - R. H. G. Way

You asked me once if I liked Italian opera.
Decades ago, a swift, negative answer fled from my lips.
It disappointed you.

I was young. An incompetent clone,
led by audio idiots - moulded by modern musical mode,
untrue to unique life form.

If I could bridge the gap, the gap of years -
the void created by ignorance, by pride, by youth,
I would answer you with honesty…

ANNETTE-FRANCES B.

Our Dream *(Composed 1976)*

Our lives we're living,
many oceans apart,
yet your spirit is with me,
it's next to my heart.

With each other to love,
with each other to hold,
we'll gather our memories,
for when we grow old.

Memories of colour,
movement and noise,
memories of children,
scattering toys.

Our lives will be lived,
each moment with meaning,
each moment of work,
each moment of dreaming.

This dream will be ours,
if you tell me you care
and our lives will be one life,
forever to share.

ANNETTE-FRANCES B.

Message from Annette

- Mother's Day 2018 -

When I was a child,
you showed me rainbows,
jumped in deep puddles beside me,
did cartwheels in the garden on a warm summer's day
and you filled my life with music, poetry and excitement.

You gave me the freedom to discover life,
to be myself,
whilst gently guiding me
to understand right from wrong
and falseness from sincerity.
You encouraged me to understand
how to be kind and to love others more than myself.

You taught me, by example,
how to love life,
have a strong sense of adventure
and a deep Christian faith.
You gave me love and understanding
and the skills needed
to be a good parent and grandparent.

Now I am older,
you continue to fill my life with love,
kindness, music, laughter and a sense of adventure.
You are and always will be,
my fantastic mother and my best friend.

ANNETTE-FRANCES B.

Our Grandma *(Composed 2018)*

Our Grandma was so many amazing things,
An actress, a dancer,
A Singer with the most wonderfully effortless voice,
She was even a kangaroo in a pantomime once!
She was a loving wife, a poet,
A mother and best friend to her daughter,
A caring and wise grandma who helped my brothers and I
To become who we are today,
She was fiercely intelligent and yet humble all at once,
But what I will always keep with me is that:
She was true to herself,
Never false and her heart was filled with a love for life and
for everyone around her.
A soul too bright and full of love to ever fade.
I will miss you dearly and hope to see you again someday.

S. A. W. BRANNON

Beautiful Spirit *(Composed 2020)*

- To my Mother -

Your beautiful spirit…
lives on, inspires, prevails and triumphs
within our hearts…
forever…

Your love,
for music and poetry,
for adventure,
for nature
and your wonderful joie de vivre,
delivered inspiration, motivation and liberation.

Your unswerving faith
in your family,
in humanity,
in God,
encouraged hope, confidence and competence.

Your beautiful spirit…
lives on, inspires, prevails and triumphs
within our hearts…
forever…

ANNETTE-FRANCES B.

The Rest is Just the Past *(Composed 2012)*

Cool waters flowing to the Sussex Sea,
The summer's sun sits lazily in the west.
The circle dance is where we want to be.
With best foot forward, we will do our best,
Then as we meet and great and leave the street,
To join the others in the friendly hall:
We read with joy, from hand-written info. sheet,
Held fast with sticky-tack on painted wall,
There is to be a meeting - circle wise.
The date is set to greet the kind full moon,
It always comes to us as no surprise,
These outings never seem to come too soon.
Now once again, the dance and music start.
Hand holding hand, while music guides the feet.
Though hands are held – it's love that holds the heart.
We glance across and with our minds we meet.
The soothing sound and movement merge and flow,
Then problems of the week are lost at last,
In peaceful silence, circle dancers know,
'The die is cast' – the rest is just the past…

DAVID KING

To Vera *(Composed 2018)*

Now, with the passing of these twenty years,
With all our joy and all our tears,
We faced it all together
You always found the way,
You are with me forever,
On this, and every day.

You are my light,
My loved one,
My partner and my friend,
I love you darling Vera.
Our love will never end.

DAVID KING

People Lanterns *(Composed 1989)*

We feel the touch of foot on wood -
Is good to feel.
'Or, so we should,'
But is this moment real?
Or do we feel:

This transient moment,
Can steal this atmosphere,
And store it in the rear
Of complex, cortex mechanism
Till yet a later year?

Now when we dance:
In unison, as one,
And some have found the sound
May hound away the stress of life,

Yet others see this as the 'flip side'
End to strife.

Now when we give to others:
All - they give to us,
Plus, the new awareness,
That with each new day,

We trust a little more,
And must a little more
Be trusted too.
But is this all so new?

Did we these complex paths traverse,
To rediscover
Ways we knew at birth?
Did earth and air hold safe
These simple truths in keeping,

Weeping for the light that burnt
In the empty house?
For all the lights were on,
But nobody was home!

Now, all of us are home,
No more to be alone.
For all the lights which shine in here:
Are People Lanterns bright and clear.

DAVID KING

Fleeting Thoughts

Now but a Memory *(Composed 1999)*

The heat of this summer's day,
Now but a memory,
As the gentle hand of evening caresses all,
And now the whispering trees their secrets tell,
While our hearts are calm with thought,
                               and shadows fall.

VERA ANNIE WEBB…NÉE WAY…

Wise Words *(Composed 1978)*

The artist's paradise is just around the corner.

This strange effigy of man,
it's all a phenomenon,
some of us are leading on.
It's all part of a great plan.

Griffin E. D. Way (Griff)

Words to granddaughter – Annette-Frances,
within final weeks of Griff's life.

Where am I and how did I get here?
(Composed 2003)

Where am I and how did I get here?
From cheetah to meerkat and back again in a moment,
from point-to-point we ride.
These points of sudden familiarity,
relationships of conscious empathy,
each unexpected comma
a doorway to the last.
We stand in retrospect,
prodding with eyes,
feeling in the dark, for the light switch,
as if to let a part of us catch up,
lighting a beacon to say: "I was here and here and now here."
The networks of comma like consciousness stretch on,
some from morning to evening,
some from lifetime to lifetime
and so off we sail,
until we meet again my friend.

ALEX LOUIS WAY BRANNON

My Hand in Yours
(Created 2020)

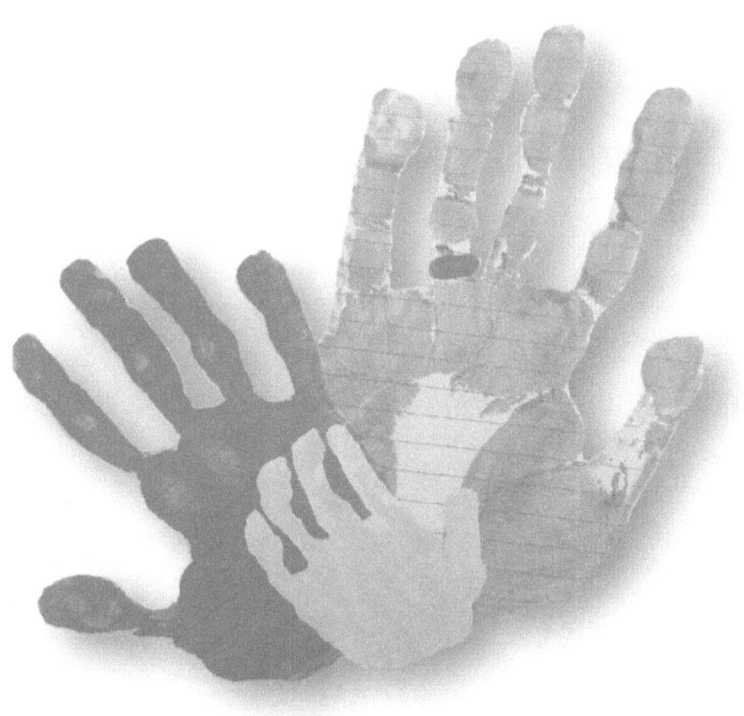

JACK RAY LOUIS BRANNON
(age 14 months)

Links Between Writers

Poems and song lyrics, within this book, represent the creative reflections of five generations, connected by marriage, partnership or parentage.

Those individuals who have contributed poems/lyrics to: "Take a Look Again…" are shown **in bold** on page 87.

Family links

Griffin Edward David Way
b. 1897   *m.* 1920
Frances Constance Binning Smith

P. O. Way (Female) *m.* A. H.	R. H. G. Way (Male) *m.* A. W.	B. D. Way (Male) *m.* H. E.	**Vera Annie Way** *b. 1935* *m.* 1956 Louis James Webb
One son		One daughter	

Annette-Frances Webb *b.* 1958
m. 1977
R. W. Brannon

Vera widowed 1996

1998
Vera & David King

Alexander Louis Way Brannon *b.* 1980 *m.* 2008 Akiko Tokunaga	**Tom Paul Way Brannon** *b.* 1982 *uncle to*	**Simon Arthur Way Brannon** *b.* 1985 *m.* 2016 **Lucy Arwen Bailey**
Ai Daisy Brannon *b.* 2011		**Jack Ray Louis Brannon** *b.* 2019

Brief Biographies

Reflecting upon this section of the book, we are aware that the first two or three biographies are somewhat longer than the rest. This is perhaps because they represent individuals whose lives have stretched over eighty or so years and subconsciously we have been reluctant to over condense their experiences, for fear of omitting points that may be of interest to future generations. The remaining biographies vary in length and this is purely dependent upon the amount of information each writer wished to share!

Griffin E. D. Way (Griff)
(*b*.1897 - *d*.1978)

Griff grew up in the Isle of Wight. He was the second of six children. Family values emphasised: compassion for humanity, honesty, kindness and respect, intertwined with music, culture, education and hard work. Eager to serve his country, during WW1, Griff joined the Royal Horse Artillery. Throughout the war, a pre-existing regard for horses, gained whilst growing up in the I.O.W., strengthened to become a lifelong respect and admiration for their loyalty and intelligence. On one occasion, whilst Griff was at the front with his horses - as they pulled along a large military gun, the horses deliberately swerved off route to avoid impending disaster, thus saving the lives of many men.

After WW1 Griff met his future wife, Connie, at a dance in Southampton. Connie had spent part of WW1, in France, working on Ordnance Survey with the Women's Army Auxiliary Core (WAAC). Comparing wartime notes the couple realised they had previously seen each other, from a distance, when Griff's battalion had passed through Wimereux and waved to a group of WAAC ladies.

In 1920, eager to earn his living in London, Griff spend three days cycling there from Southampton, stopping only for food and rest. Ultimately, he and Connie married, bought a house in Surrey and raised four children. With strong compassion for his fellow man, Griff once offered a temporary home, to a homeless gentleman, who promptly robbed the family silver overnight! Undaunted, a few years later, Griff felt compassion for an elderly, confused gentleman and gave him food and shelter. Via a newspaper ad, he discovered the gentleman was a retired vicar, recently widowed and suffering from amnesia. The gentleman's worried daughter was contacted and the pair were happily reunited.

Throughout his life, Griff enjoyed music. He played the violin; plus, he and Connie sang in philharmonic choirs in Surrey and later in Hampshire. He was often voted as Choir Secretary and did much voluntary work for local organisations. In addition, he was a wise, guiding light and vibrant, positive influence upon his children and grandchildren.

Vera Annie Webb - Née Way (*b*.1935 - *d*.2018)

As a child Vera attended many classical music events in Surrey, with her parents. Her mother played the piano, her father the violin and both parents sang. Vera sang beautifully, recited poetry, enjoyed piano lessons and persuaded her parents to allow her to attend ballet, drama and singing lessons. She also liked climbing trees!

Despite being considered a talented academic student, Vera was impatient to experience life away from the classroom. After school, each day, she continued her music and drama studies and performed in amateur shows. Her dream was to become a professional singer. After several auditions and whilst still within her final weeks at grammar school, Vera was offered a part in a professional production. Although she had secured a scholarship, to one of London's leading music colleges, Vera opted instead to travel with the theatrical company and experience the university of life! Ultimately, she achieved a good reputation as a singer and toured throughout England, Ireland, Scotland and Wales.

In 1952, whilst on theatrical tour, Vera stood watching a sensational adagio act as they rehearsed. One of the dancers, a dark-haired male, Louis, looked in her direction. Their eyes met and that was the beginning of a whole new chapter in Vera's life. Vera and Louis married in 1956 and had one daughter in 1958.

Widowed in 1996, Vera slowly rebuilt her life: she helped her Church, taught drama in a local nursery, did readings for the 'Talking Newspaper for the Blind' - spent time with her grandchildren, wrote poems for an anthology, joined two choirs and travelled to Canada.

In 1998, Vera met her kindred spirit, David, at choir practice. The pair spent the rest of Vera's life together. In addition to voluntary and choir work, in England, Vera travelled to Malaysia each Autumn, meeting with David to spend a few weeks absorbing and contributing to life in Penang. Whilst in Penang, each Autumn and Winter, she and David taught English in a local school and helped a Stroke Association, by running music therapy sessions; plus, sang with two Malaysian choirs. Whenever Vera had time she wrote poems.

David King (*b*.1937)

David's poems have been published in a range of magazines, throughout the years. Originally from London, he has two grown up children and two teenage grandchildren.

For many years, following retirement, David spent Autumn and Winter living and doing voluntary work in Penang (Malaysia). Along with his partner Vera, he sang in choirs, taught English and provided music therapy sessions for a stroke association. David's partner, Vera, had a huge sense of adventure, combined with a very happy nature; hence, the couple often used to catch the overnight train to Thailand, where they enjoyed back packing. Both were sad to see so many homeless in Thailand and Vera always gave them food or money. The couple would return, from Malaysia, each year, to sing in their Sussex choirs and spend time with family and friends.

In 2003 David was asked to do a month's voluntary work, with a school in Yangon (Burma). He taught approximately a hundred adult students, all within one hall. The work was demanding, but rewarding.

On December 26th, 2004 – the day of the deadly Tsunami – nations mourned the disaster and many people, like David, felt a desperate need to be of some use. Having a huge respect for the work of the Global Sikh's, David asked if he could be granted the privilege of utilising previous training, to help them - perhaps as a medical assistant. After written and verbal vetting, David flew over Banda Aceh and witnessed the terrible devastation – paddy fields and farms totally submerged. Living onboard a sailing ship, he worked alongside Dr's, helping the injured in the remaining villages. He was later asked to help in a hospital in Sabang.

David cared for Vera, throughout her long battle with Cancer, ultimately remaining in England from 2014 - 2018, but managing to do some English teaching online. He still teaches online, writes poems, plays the cello, sings in a choir and helps a number of elderly neighbours; plus, spends time with his family.

Annette-Frances B. (*b*.1958)

Annette-Frances B's (A. F./Nettie) first poem was published, in a children's magazine, when she was just ten. Using a succession of pen names, A. F. has contributed her poems, to a fairly diverse range of books and magazines.

As a child A. F. thrived within a happy, loving family, where music, poetry, travel and adventure were valued and embraced. Her mother gave up her career, as a professional singer, when A. F. was three, but never stopped singing – in the house, in choirs and even as they walked along the beach! A. F.'s father, originally a professional adagio dancer, told wonderful theatrical tales, quoted Shakespeare and used to act out various scenes from Shakespearean plays.

As an adult A. F. ran a nursery school and lectured in colleges. She is married, has three grown up children and two lively grandchildren. A. F. adores adventure, travel, running on the beach with her dog, music, poetry and white water rafting. In recent years, she has written two poetry books for children and one lively rhyming story.

R. W. Brannon (*b*.1954)

A keen illustrator, R. W. Brannon enjoys observing and sketching mini-beasts, reptiles and other small creatures, often turning his sketches into humorous cartoons. His skills have been used to design logos and business leaflets.

R. W.'s a proud father and grandfather; plus, adores travel and music. In recent years he's been diagnosed with Parkinson's disease, but has risen to the challenge by utilising each 'good day' as fully as possible. He has illustrated three books, written a few poems, enjoys meditation, creates interesting recipes, does Tai Chi in his local swimming pool and has started to teach himself the five-string banjo.

Alex Louis Way Brannon (*b.*1980)

Alex's earlier writing includes a booklet of poems, published in 2003. Recently (2019) he completed a children's adventure story and is now working on a second one.

Alex has travelled far from his original career, as an art lecturer. In 2006 he and his Japanese girlfriend, Akiko (Aki), decided to backpack around Europe. They did voluntary work in exchange for food and accommodation. Projects included: helping to build an echo-house in the Czech Republic; plus, pottery demos and workshops in various European towns and villages. Whilst in Switzerland - in the famous Jungfraujoch 'Ice Palace' - Alex dropped to one knee and proposed to Aki, amidst much clapping from other tourists!

The couple settled in Japan, for several years, where Alex was made welcome by Aki's family. Swiftly he adapted to and embraced the Japanese culture. He worked for a language school; plus taught English in a large Junior High School. Daughter, Ai, was born in Fukuoka in 2011.

Having returned to Europe, to be closer to family in England, Alex and Aki now run an online language training centre. In his spare time Alex keeps active with exercise, leather work, helping his local church and writing.

A. D. Brannon - aged 8 (*b.* 2011)

A. D. Brannon (Ai) is our youngest contributor of poetry, at just eight years old! As an avid bookworm, Ai has worked her way through numerous large volumes of children's classics, modern fantasy and adventure stories; plus, non-fiction books on nature and the universe, so it seems natural that she now likes to write down some of her own thoughts and ideas. Other hobbies include ballet, jazz, drama, piano lessons, wildlife and messy creative craft; plus, speaking online with her cousins and great grandma in Japan.

Tom B.
(*b.* 1982)

Tom B. is a writer and illustrator. His illustrations are especially dynamic and almost impossible to ignore. As a writer his work includes song lyrics and these have been of interest to musicians, especially local Sussex musicians. The following link may be of interest: www.reverbnation.com/richardcampbell
Tom B. is a popular uncle to his young niece and nephew, both of whom enjoy his wicked sense of humour and ability to understand and entertain them.

S. A. W. Brannon & L. A. Brannon
(*both b.*1985)

S. A. W. Brannon (Simon) and L. A. Brannon (Lucy) met at drama college in 2002. They became friends and later fell in love, whilst practising lines together. They married in 2016 and have a wonderfully lively, baby son, Jack. Born in 2019, Jack has transformed their world. He is a constant source of joy and interest and as he strives towards each new skill, his own, unique character unfolds a little more, lighting the lives of those who observe him.

INDEX OF WRITERS

Griffin E. D. Way (*b.* Isle of Wight, UK, 1897)
28, 29, 30, 83

Vera Annie Webb - Née Way (*b.* Surrey, UK 1935—2018)
12, 13, 16, 17, 18, 19, 26, 30, 31, 39, 69, 83

David King (b. London, UK 1937)
62, 63, 64, 65, 70, 71, 79, 80, 81

Annette-Frances B. - Née Webb (*b.* London, UK 1958)
15, 16, 38, 45, 46, 47, 51, 52, 53, 67, 74, 75, 76, 78

R. W. Brannon (*b.* Essex, UK 1954)
8, 9, 27, 59, 60, 61, 72,

Alex Louis Way Brannon (*b.* Cambridgeshire, UK 1980)
1, 2, 3, 4, 5, 6, 7, 8, 22, 23, 25, 48, 49, 66, 67, 84

Tom B. (*b.* Cambridgeshire, UK 1982)
10, 11, 32, 33, 34, 35, 36, 37, 41, 42, 43, 54, 55, 56, 57 58

S. A. W. Brannon (*b.* E. Sussex, UK 1985)
44, 45, 73, 77,

L. A. Brannon - Née Bailey (*b.* Kent 1985)
72,

A. D. Brannon (*b.* Fukuoka, Japan, 2011)
20, 21

Jack Ray Louis Brannon (*b.* Kent, 2019)
85 (Pictorial)

INDEX OF TITLES & FIRST LINES

Titles are in *italic*. If the first line is the same as the title, then only the first line will be written.

A fictitious man, though he's "carried the can" 28
A gust of breeze stirs the trees 15
A Momentary Snapshot 5
A proud young manager, named Jay, 51
All the people in the world 31
Always Purchase Your Car Tax on Time 52
And so, you've heard it all before 43
Angry faces – Seeking utopia in a hostile mechanical city. 47
As Morning Tones 66
Beat down revolutions of the drum 54
Beautiful Spirit 78
Before You Know it, You're Somewhere Else 4
Betrayer's Voice 32
Blackbird there upon the post, 17
Capture the moment in time 8
Carve the world up, for ease of manipulation… 7
Cliché 43
Cool waters flowing to the Sussex Sea, 79
Dandelions and Buttercups 18
Directional Hard Work 56
Do you Like Italian Opera? 74
Favourite Place 16
First Flat – Somewhere in Muswell Hill 67
Fleeting Glimpse – Port of Calais, Summer 2015 47
Forgotten 15
General War 28
How can state be different 5
Hypocrite Boogie 44
I close my eyes, for a second 4

I often seem to invent things by accident 63
I soaked my feet, then brushed my hair 52
I Think About the World 39
If I cast my thoughts asunder 56
 If I Lived a Million Times 73
Inventions 63
 Just a tumble-down flat, with an outside loo, 67
Life 12
Life is a wonderful thing, 12
 Little Bird 16
Little wildflowers, golden, bright, 18
Long ago, I really thought it could be done, 30
Look Into the Eyes of Humanity 27
Mercury is slightly appealing, 20
Message from Annette 76
Money holds no respect here, 48
Morning Awakes 15
My Hand in Yours (pictorial) 85
My One and Only Vera 71
No space for time 10
Nobody in the world will ever make me 72
Now but a Memory 83
Now, with the passing of these twenty years, 80
Nuclear Weapons – War… 38
Oasis 1
Of all the things I love about you, 71
Oh, what love I have for the woman in my life, 72
Omega 45
On a Summer's day… 13
Our Dream 75
Our Grandma 77
Our Grandma was so many amazing things, 77
Our lives we're living, many oceans apart, 75
Paradox 64

Paradox...What is it? 64
Parted 69
People 31
People Lanterns 80
Poetical Reflections* 70
Raging banshee wail of survival 35
Resolutions 62
S**t Kickers Bargain Bucket 10
Shopping with Parkinson's disease can cause chaos... 59
Sights and Sounds I Love 17
So still the trees 19
So, this is it – this great abyss. 45
Song - Let's Find Love – 26
Still Moving I Sat 22
Suit keeps face where a smile is placed. 41
Summer Thoughts 13
Supermarket Chaos 59
Survival of the Fittest 48
Take a Look Again 2
The artist's paradise is just around the corner. This strange 83
The heat of this summer's day, 83
The Manager Saves the Day 51
The powerful, eternal waves, 16
The Rest is Just the Past 79
The story of a child with eyes so wild 44
The truth is there, look into their eyes... 27
There are jewels, of every colour, in the blink of every eye. 25
There he lives his little life, 16
Thermo nuclear twister 35
To my Father 74
To Vera 80
Toast to Our Love 72
Vicious Cycle 54
We all stop counting after a while 2
We all walk the desert 1

We Cannot Change the World 30
We did not know, blindly we did not see... 69
We feel the touch of foot on wood, 80
Welcome to the GAHC! 41
Well, did Kipling say it all?* 70
What have you done to my world, 38
What If? 20
What is... 7
When I was a child. you showed me rainbows, 76
When we try to make these things, 62
Where am I and how did I get here? 84
Where is Time if Not Forgotten? 8
Why? 25
Winter Scene 19
Wise Words 83
You amaze me 73
You asked me once if I liked Italian opera. 74
You gotta shoot the dice 32
Young hands, resting on old hands, 74
Your beautiful spirit... 78

*Poets acknowledged and quoted, within "Poetical Reflections" - page 70 - are available within the public domain.

Louannvee Publishing
www.louannveepublishing.co.uk

www.ingramcontent.com/pod-product-compliance
Lightning Source LLC
Chambersburg PA
CBHW030453010526
44118CB00011B/922